Easy and Enjoyable
Driving Your Horse

An introduction to training your horse to drive,
preparing for breed show driving and participating
in American Driving Society driving.

Driving Your Horse

First Publish 1989, Reprinted 1997 & 2022
Copyright © 2022 by Equine Heritage Institute, Inc.

All rights reserved. No part of this publication may be reproduced, distributed, or transmitted in any form or by any means, including photocopying, recording, or other electronic or mechanical methods, without the prior written permission of the publisher, except in the case of brief quotations embodied in critical reviews and certain other noncommercial uses permitted by copyright law. For permission requests, write to the publisher, addressed "Attention: Permissions Coordinator," at the address below.

Equine Heritage Institute, Inc.
3024 Marion County Road Weirsdale, FL 32195
Office: (352) 753-2826 Fax: (352) 753-6186

ISBN: 978-1-951895-22-8

TABLE OF CONTENTS

11 Preface
   12 Comparison of Driving Styles *(Figure 8)*
14 Starting Guidelines
   14 Prior Training
   14 Age
   15 Home Base
   16 Getting Your Horse's Attention
   18 Communication with Your Horse in Harness *(Figure 1,2,3,6)*
   22 Voice Commands
   23 Voice Reprimands, Praise
   24 Bit and Reins *(Figure 5,7)*
   29 Whip
32 Training in Ten Steps
   32 Step One: Fitting the Harness
   37 Step Two: Ground Driving – Moving Forward
   40 Step Three: Ground Driving – Stopping & Standing
   41 Step Four: Ground Driving – Turning
   44 Step Five: Ground Driving – Attaching the Cart *(Figure 4)*
   49 Step Six: Ground Driving – Pulling & Holding Back
   50 Practicing Ground Driving at Roadside

51 Step Seven: Entering the Cart
53 Step Eight: Trotting on Straightaway & Turns
55 Step Nine: Varying Gaits – Extension & Collection
56 Step Ten: Backing
58 Pleasure of Driving Your Horse

59 Appendix
　　Selected Contacts for Further Information

Illustrations

Figure 1: Driving Bridle - pg 18, 35
Figure 2: Typical Breed Show Harness - pg 19, 33
Figure 3: American Driving Society Harness - pg 20, 34, 42
Figure 4: Attaching the Harness & Cart - pg 46
Figure 5: Types of Bits - pg 26
Figure 6: Types of Whips - pg 21
Figure 7: Holding the Reins & Whip - pg 27, 31
Figure 8: Comparison of Driving Styles - pg 12

ACKNOWLEDGEMENTS

I am grateful to many individuals who assisted in the production of this booklet, so you could benefit from our experiences with Nature's most beautiful animal-- the horse.

Gloria Austin, 1986

Don Grentzinger, trainer, Brockport, New York, for his kind remarks in discussing the technical aspects of training horses.

Sue Olds, Farm Manager at Mendon Equestrian Center, for her skill in caring for and training our horses.

Karen Swartz, Linda Beaulieu, Earle Billington, and Chel Chave for their willingness to share their knowledge and skills. Thanks also go to Martha White of Island Akita & Miniature Horses.

And to Rajah, Silver Flash, Top Gun, Bingo, Misty, Dream and the many other horses at Mendon Equestrian Center for the countless hours of enjoyment we have shared with them.

- *Gloria Austin*

PREFACE

This booklet is designed for use in training your horse to drive. We recommend you read the entire booklet before deciding if you have the skill to train your own horse. Remember, horses are creatures of habit. It takes great patience and continued repetition to train a horse to drive. Be prepared to spend time with your horse in a variety of situations. The horse is an animal that takes flight when afraid, so you must take the time for it to develop trust in you and it new tasks. In any case, if you have problems, consult your professional trainer for assistance.

The booklet can be taken to the training area for reference while training. Figure 8 offers a chart comparing three differing styles of horse driving. We recommend you attend Breed shows and American Driving Society (ADS) competitions to observe these differences in customs and the ever-changing practices of the particular presentations.

Whether you train your horse to drive or employ a professional trainer, the information in this booklet will be helpful in driving your horse.

COMPARISON OF DRIVING STYLES

Figure #8

Be sure to check breed associations and the American Driving Society (ADS) for changes in rules and customs.

ASPECT	BREED SHOW	ROADSTER	AMER. DRIVING SOC.
Horse	Attractive; characteristic of breed	Snappy knee action and extended stride	Attractive; sturdy
Bit	Half cheek snaffle (best used with check rein)	Half cheek snaffle or other type (best used with check rein)	Liverpool, double ring snaffle, or other driving bits
Harness	Lightweight with patent leather accent	Lightweight: fine	Medium weight; sturdy with brass accents
Breeching	None	None	Yes
Check Rein	Over check or side check	Over check	Side check or none
Martingale	Optional	Optional	None

ASPECT	BREED SHOW	ROADSTER	AMER. DRIVING SOC.
Gaits	Names for gaits vary with breed: walk, collected/regular trot, working/road trot (extended)	Slow jog; road gait; drive-on ("Show your horse")	Walk; slow trot (collected); working trot; strong trot (extended)
Rein Back (Backing on command)	Depends on breed's show rules	No	Yes
Cart	Wire- or wooden-wheeled with basket	Wire-wheeled with stirrups but no basket	Wooden-wheeled; 19th Century style
Whip	Short Lash	Short Lash	Long Lash
Holding Reins	One- or two-handed	Two-handed	One- or two-handed
Dress	Stylish and appropriate to either day or evening	Similar to racing silks; colorful cap and jacket to match	Conservative; long sleeves; suit for man; hat, gloves, driving apron

DRIVING YOUR HORSE

The following is a ten-step program used for training horses to drive. After reading through this booklet, many of you will feel confident enough to commence with the training of your own horse. If however, you have doubts or meet with problems, do not hesitate to turn to a professional who has trained horses to drive.

STARTING GUIDELINES

PRIOR TRAINING
We assume the horse to be trained to drive is already leading and standing quietly when haltered. It is also advisable to have lunged your horse while using voice commands. There are many good books available on lunging.

AGE
The horse to be trained should be at least two years old, preferably three. The bones of a horse are not sufficiently developed for driving prior to age two. At age three, the horse's mind has greater maturity to learn new tasks.

HOME BASE

When training, use a "home base." In other words, **take your horse to the same area each training session.** Tie and harness the horse at the home location. Return to this location to remove the harness. Before returning the horse to the pasture or stall, brush and / or bathe (depending on the weather) the horse, as well as pick the horse's feet free of stones, in this same place. This "home base" routine is important in helping the horse feel secure in its new tasks. **Be as consistent as possible in these starting and concluding procedures.**

GETTING YOUR HORSE'S ATTENTION

When training a horse, insist on good behavior. The horse must pay strict attention to its handler. It is not a time for playing or eating. If the horse paws the ground, reprimand him or her by saying **"QUIT"** in a sharp voice. Tap or strike the horse on the leg with a crop if he continues to paw.

During a training session, the horse should not lower its head for any reason, particularly not to eat. If its head goes down while working, say **"HEAD UP"** in a sharp, stern voice. If the horse fails to pick his head up, lightly kick the horse in the back of the jaw with your hard soled shoe at the same time you say **"HEAD UP."** Learning the commands "QUIT" and "HEAD UP" will be helpful later when you are communicating with your horse from the carriage.

Do not feel that it is cruel to expect your horse to pay attention to you when you are working around him or her. There is plenty of time to play and eat outside of the training session. A horse must pay attention to and obey the handler to achieve good performance and safe driving.

If does not hurt to **leave your horse tied for a while** to learn patience and how to stand quietly. Therefore, do not feel rushed to harness or hitch your horse. Harness horses often have to stand quietly in harness for long periods of time while waiting for the next class at shows or while waiting for the parade to start, etc.

It is best to **reprimand stallions** with "QUIT" for even whinnying when being handled or under harness. Stallions, most of all, need to learn that there is a time for work and a time for breeding. You may need to reinforce "QUIT" with a jerk on a chain over the nose. *Stallions must be obedient when handled and when under harness.* Always keep stallions from nosing, touching, or bumping other horses when working with them.

COMMUNICATION WITH YOUR HORSE IN HARNESS

So that you can fully understand what follows, become familiar with Figures 1, 2, 3 and 6 (the harness and bridle) before continuing.

DRIVING BRIDLE
Figure #1

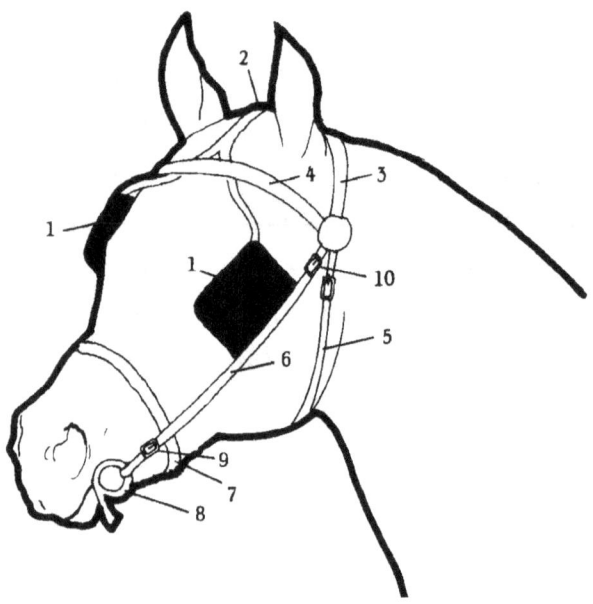

1. Blinker (Binder)
2. Blinker Stay Adjustment
3. Crown
4. Browband
5. Throatlatch
6. Cheekstrap
7. Noseband (Cavesson)
8. Driving Snaffle Bit
9. Driving Bit Adjustment
10. Blinker Adjustment

TYPICAL BREED SHOW HARNESS
Figure #2

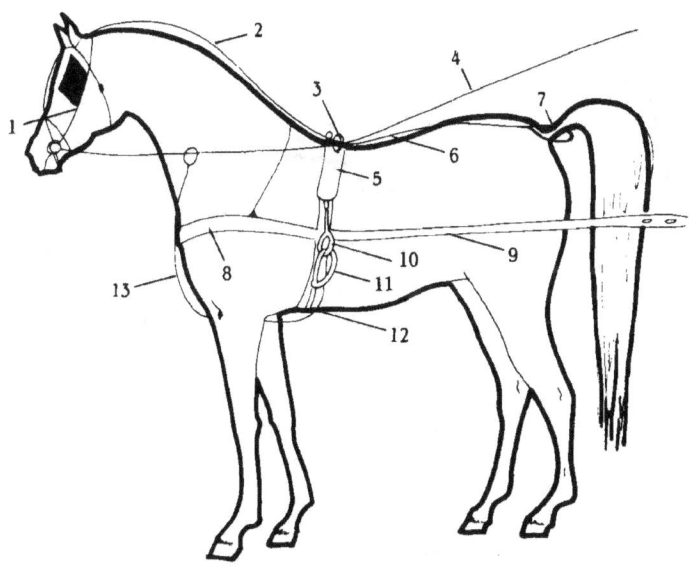

1. Bridle
2. Over Cheek
3. Rein turret
4. Rein
5. Backpad
6. Back Strap
7. Crupper
8. Breatcollar
9. Trace
10. Shaft Loop
11. Hold Down (Wrap) Strap
12. Belly Band (Surcingle)
13. Running Martingale

AMERICAN DRIVING SOCIETY HARNESS
Figure #3

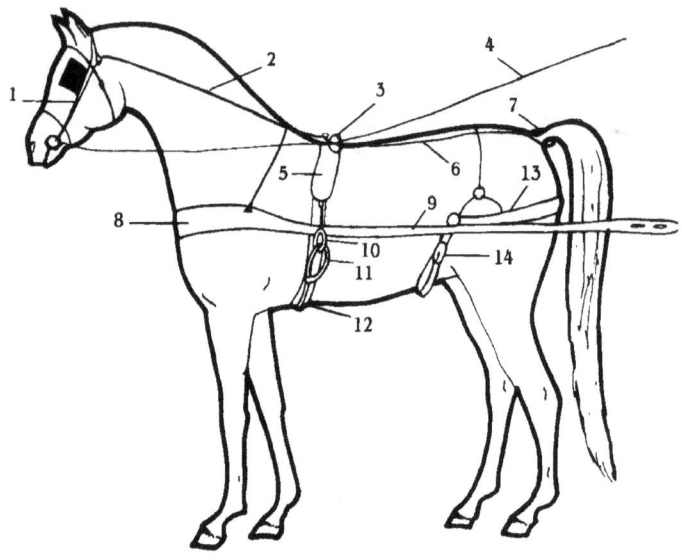

1. Bridle
2. Side Check
3. Rein turret
4. Rein
5. Backpad
6. Back Strap
7. Crupper
8. Breastcollar
9. Trace
10. Shaft Loop
11. Hold Down (Wrap) Strap
12. Belly Band (Surcingle)
13. Breeching
14. Holdback or Breeching Strap

TYPES OF WHIPS
Figure #6

A whip with the lash long enough to touch the horse's shoulder is recommended for training.

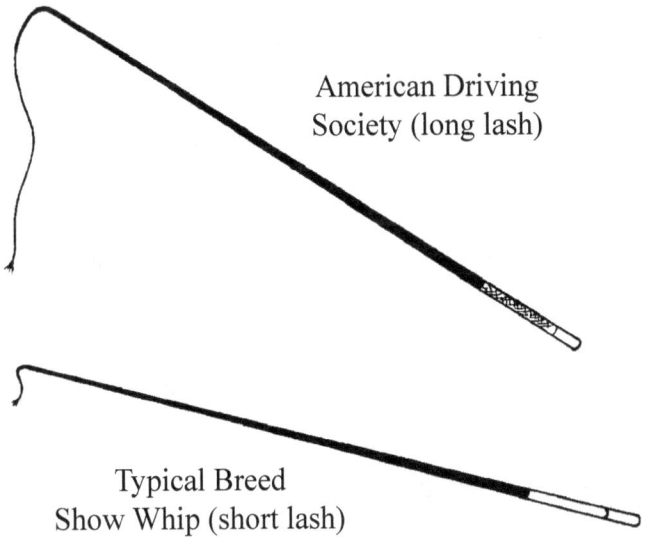

American Driving Society (long lash)

Typical Breed Show Whip (short lash)

With a driving horse you only have three ways to communicate: by **voice, bit and whip.** Compared to the saddle horse (where your body and legs indicate your presence and desires), the driving horse takes its direction from your voice and contact with its mouth through the bit and the reins. This is the only way your horse knows where you are and what you want, because it cannot feel your weight or see you when it is wearing driving blinkers.

A. VOICE

Correct use of voice is very important when training a new horse. You must get your horse to understand basic commands, praise, and reprimands through changes in your voice intonation. When you talk to your horse, **keep your voice low in tone**: a high, shrill voice will excite the horse. If a horse understands voice commands while in halter, you can more easily get it to have the same response when you are in your cart.

"Its is very helpful," according to a fellow trainer, " if the horse understands English." Of course, you can train in any language, but do be consistent.

Each command should have its own distinct sound. For example, "Whoa" and "No" sound too much alike. Therefore, we use "Quit" when we want a horse not to paw. Using words that sound alike may confuse the horse and you may not get the desired response. And because it is so important that the horse distinguish your commands be sure you avoid chattering at your horse or using excessive repetition of commands or praise.

Any horse should know its own name. If you advance to pair or four-in-hand driving, you must use the horse's name with a command to get the individual horse to respond.

Basic Voice Commands:
  a) Whoa   d) Trot   g) Stand
  b) Walk   e) Walk-on   h) Easy
  c) Come around   f) Trot-on   i) Back

Some trainers use a cluck or kissing sound to ask for movement forward. In addition to the recommended commands above, you might have others that you wish to use. Just remember, be consistent for optimal response.

Words of Reprimand:
  a) Head Up   b) Quit   c) Stop

Words of reprimand should be spoken sharply and sternly, just as commands, and should become more sharply and sternly spoken if not obeyed.

Words of Praise:
a) Good Boy/Girl   b) O.K., (name)   c) Nice

Since young, as well as older horses, need reassurance and praise when they do things correctly, develop a vocabulary of praise. So the horse receives a soothing signal to tell it of a task well done, you want to use pleasant and soft voice intonations.

Voice commands are apt to have a personal style which differ from trainer to trainer. If you send your horse to a professional trainer, learn what voice commands and what voice intonations were used in the training process. We also recommend that you initially drive your horse under the professional trainer's supervision, for it is essential to be as consistent as possible with verbal commands.

B. BITS & REINS

The bit and reins play a very important part in communication with the horse. With an educated horse, **subtle movement of the rein** and the resulting action on the bit **will cue the horse** to move on, slow down, and turn. Consistent responses, however, come only after many hours of training.

Many styles of bits are available (see Figure 5 for the most common bits). The bit must be properly fitted to the width of the horse's mouth. Make sure the joints of the bit do not pinch the horse's mouth. The bit should ride over the top of the horse's tongue, high in its mouth, but not stretching the corners more than a wrinkle.

When first training a horse, it is **important for the horse to get used to the bit.** Some trainers will put a bridle and bit on the horse (without reins and blinkers) and leave it on the horse in the stall so the horse can become accustomed to the feel of the bit in the mouth. The horse will chew on the bit and move it around in its mouth until comfortable with this strange, new thing. A young horse may even put its tongue over the top of the bit. All of this is normal; do not get too worried. Eventually the horse will accept the bit and not move it around.

When using the bit to cue a driving horse, it is important to "maintain contact" with the horse's mouth when the horse is moving. This means to hold the reins tautly enough to feel the horse's mouth in your fingers. The taut but not too taut contact, along with your voice, are the only ways the horse feels your presence.

TYPES OF BITS
Figure #5

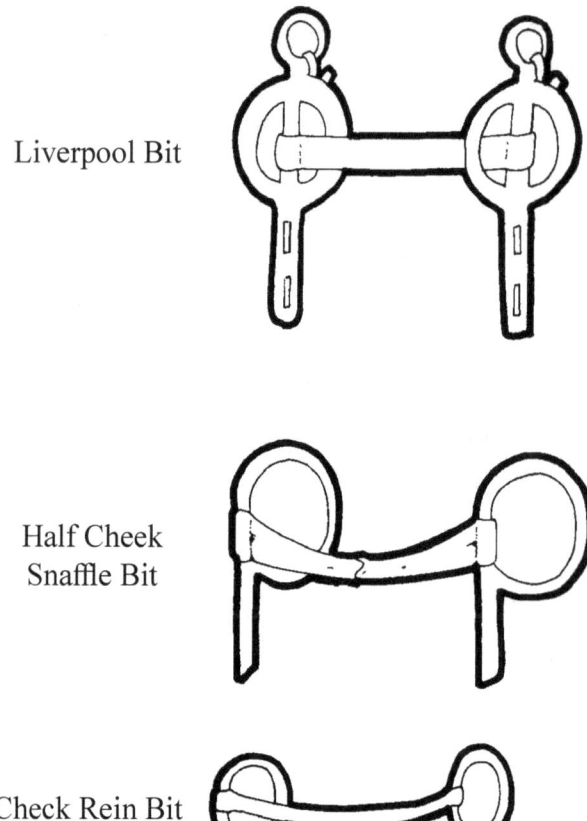

Liverpool Bit

Half Cheek
Snaffle Bit

Check Rein Bit

Before you attempt to train your horse, practice holding and manipulating the reins. There are many ways of handling reins; different styles are used in different driving situations. We recommend training with the use of one of the methods where **both reins are held in the left hand** (see Figure 7), while the right hand (which is also holding the whip) is used to draw up or release each rein as needed.

HOLDING THE REIN AND WHIP
Figure #7

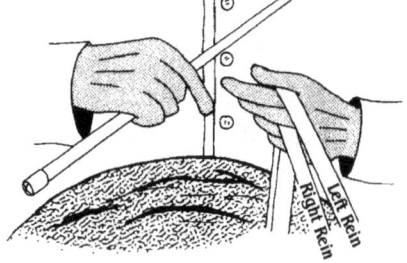

English Style

Hungarian Method

When driving a horse, we use a rein maneuver called **"half-halts"**. Half-halts are achieved by gently squeezing and releasing the fingers which hold the rein. When stopping, use half-halts with both reins. **When turning, use a half-halt on the rein on the side of the turn, at the same time that you relax the rein on the opposite side.** With this combination of rein pressure, the horse is free to turn its head in the desired direction before it steps in the direction of the turn. Keep half-halting the horse to that direction until the body also moves in the direction of the turn. Then use verbal praise and release some of the rein pressure. Eventually your horse will move in the direction of the turn with light, steady rein pressure on the side of the turn.

After you apply pressure to the horse's mouth **when asking for a halt,** and the horse stops, **release the pressure as a reward** for complying with your request. If the horse stands quietly, there is no need to keep a taut rein. Just **make sure that your reins are not so slack that they might get caught on a shaft of the cart while** your horse is standing. The horse should also be reprimanded for lowering its head when standing. If the horse lowers its head, the reins and / or check rein* can get caught under the shaft which **could lead to disaster.**

*The purpose of the check rein is to hold the horse's head in an elevated position.

When you get ready to **move forward (or backward) after standing** it is important to give your horse some cue that you are going to be **asking for movement.** The primary way of doing this is to take up the slack in your reins and get contact with the horse's mouth. Some people use terms such as "Head Up." "O.K.," or "Ready" followed by a cluck or the word "Walk" (or the word "Back"). Unlike a practice used with draft horses, we never slap the horse with the reins. This disturbs the essential line of communication through the reins from you to your horse's mouth.

C. WHIP

The whip can be viewed as a replacement for a rider's legs on a saddle horse. Both the whip and the legs aid in communicating commands to get your horse to bend and move forward. You and your horse should **never view the whip as an instrument of torture or cruelty,** but as a device for communication, since you are not sitting on its back. Consequently, a positive and sensitive introduction of the whip to your horse is crucial so that the whip does not become associated with fear or pain. One way of accomplishing this is by affectionately stroking the horse all over its body with the whip.

At the outset of training, we try to train the horse to the voice and / or a cluck. As training progresses and more encouragement is needed, a tap by the whip* above the trace and behind the backpack on either side of the horse's body (where your legs would fall on a saddle horse) is appropriate.

Another whip signal is used to **achieve greater forward impulsion.** Tap the horse behind the belly band below the trace (approximately where the heel of a rider would be if the horse were mounted).

We strongly recommend that you learn one of the methods of holding both reins in your left hand, so that your **right hand is free to use**

the whip as an aid (see Figure 7). When you hold the whip in the same hand you are using to hold one of the reins, you lose contact with the horse's mouth when using the whip. This makes it difficult for the horse to understand what you want during the training phase.

In our own training, we prefer to use a long lash whip that is long enough to reach the horse's shoulder.

HOLDING THE REIN AND WHIP
Figure #7

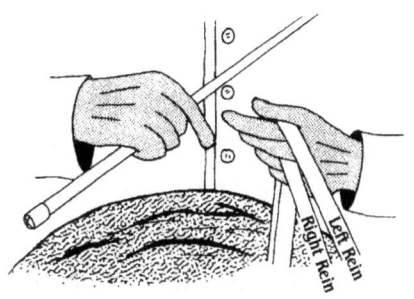

English Style

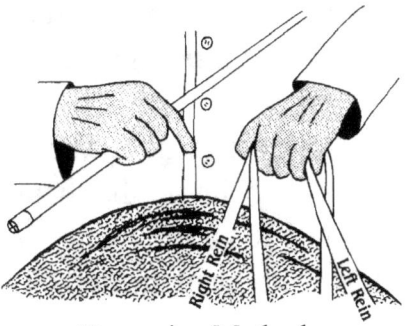

Hungarian Method

TRAINING IN TEN STEPS

The following steps for training may be viewed as daily sessions. Be advised that some horses may move through these steps quickly while others may take longer. You may need to repeat a step for a few sessions or days before moving on. If you have problems, consult a professional trainer.

STEP ONE: FITTING THE HARNESS
(see Figures 1, 2, 3)

Fit the harness to the horse and make all necessary adjustments. The **backpad** and **crupper** go on first. Make sure that all hairs are out from between the tail and crupper. The strap between the crupper and the backpad is called the back strap; it should be taut but not so taut as to elevate the tail when the horse is a rest. The **belly band** (surcingle) should be snug, but not as tight as when securing a saddle.

The **breast collar** goes on next. The breast collar must rest across the points of the shoulder, but not so high as to interfere with breathing by restricting the windpipe at the base of the neck. The breast collar must not be allowed to ride below the point of the shoulder because it can interfere with

TYPICAL BREED SHOW HARNESS
Figure #2

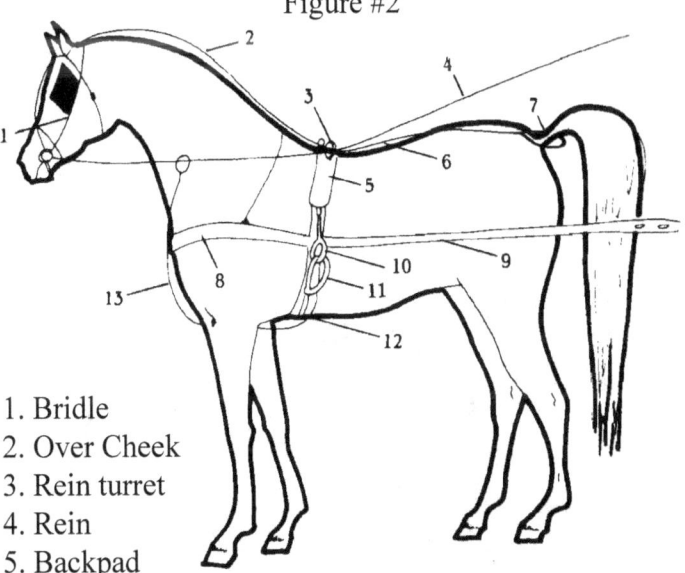

1. Bridle
2. Over Cheek
3. Rein turret
4. Rein
5. Backpad
6. Back Strap
7. Crupper
8. Breatcollar
9. Trace
10. Shaft Loop
11. Hold Down (Wrap) Strap
12. Belly Band (Surcingle)
13. Running Martingale

extension of the front legs. (Roadster turnouts require the breast collar to be slightly higher so as not to interfere with shoulder action.)

The **breeching** goes on next and should fit below the point of the rump, but not so low as to interfere with rear leg action. (Later when the cart is attached, be watchful that the breeching does not ride up toward the crupper as the cart is held back by the horse.)

AMERICAN DRIVING SOCIETY HARNESS
Figure #3

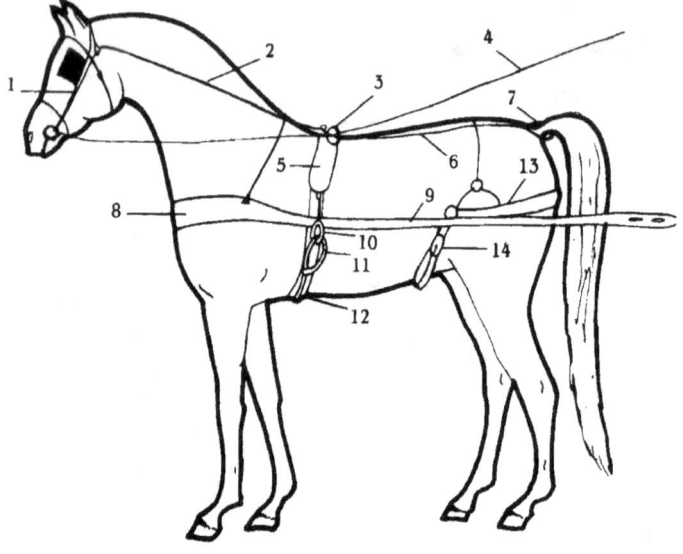

1. Bridle
2. Side Check
3. Rein turret
4. Rein
5. Backpad
6. Back Strap
7. Crupper
8. Breastcollar
9. Trace
10. Shaft Loop
11. Hold Down (Wrap) Strap
12. Belly Band (Surcingle)
13. Breeching
14. Holdback or Breeching Strap

The cart will not be used in training until Step 5. For now, **secure the traces** so they do not drag on the ground. With a full-size horse the traces may be wrapped into the breeching straps; with a miniature the traces may be laid under the back strap across the back of the horse.

Leave the halter on the horse for the first few days of training, because you are required to lead the horse on occasion. We do not recommend a **check rein** during the first few days, since it is too confining for a new horse. We reprimand the horse for lowering his head at any time with a voice command instead of relying on the check rein.

The **bit** should be set high in the mouth but should not stretch the corners more than a wrinkle. A **noseband** or cavesson is recommended to help the horse keep his mouth closed on the bit. The **cheekstrap** should be adjusted so the horse's eyes are centered in the blinkers.

DRIVING BRIDLE
Figure #1

1. Blinker (Binder)
2. Blinker Stay Adjustment
3. Crown
4. Browband
5. Throatlatch
6. Cheekstrap
7. Noseband (Cavesson)
8. Driving Snaffle Bit
9. Driving Bit Adjustment
10. Blinker Adjustment

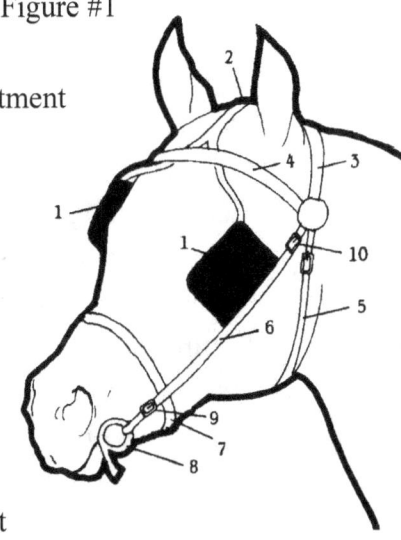

Just like having a "home base," it is good to have a **regular work area** in which to conduct the training sessions. Use as wide of an arena as possible to minimize tight turns in the early steps of training. It is very important to work in an enclosed area like an arena or paddock.

In this first stage of training your horse to drive, **lead your horse** so that it can get used to the feel of all the straps, the blinkers and the crupper. When we lead the horse in harness, we use the command words **"walk" and "whoa."**

Lead your horse all around your designated work area, starting and stopping time and time again to the words "walk" and "whoa".

It is very, very important that your horse know the work "whoa" and will stop perfectly still on this command. If the horse does not stop quickly and completely, repeat the word sharply and snap the lead line at the same time. If you ever get in trouble with a horse in harness, you will know the importance of this command. Do no wait until then to **teach your horse thoroughly the meaning of "whoa".**

STEP TWO: GROUND DRIVING
Moving Forward

Harness your horse at the "home base" again and repeat the leading exercise using the words "walk" and "whoa."

Attach the driving reins now. After attaching the reins to the bit, put the reins through the rein terrets. Have your horse stand in the "whoa" position. Then walk behind the horse to ground drive. Ground driving is a procedure in which the trainer stays on the ground and walks behind the horse to drive it. (Ground driving is done without the cart at this step; at Step 5 the cart is added. Only at Step 7 does the trainer actually ride in the cart.)

As you begin ground driving, it may be helpful to use an assistant to lead your horse initially. The assistant should take a less active role as the horse becomes comfortable with direction from you as ground driver.

At this stage of training, your horse is usually very insecure walking out there **with no one beside it.** It may try to walk up to, touch, or stop by a fence, bush, or another person or horse. Try to keep your horse a reasonable distance from such objects so it will not stop by them. Your horse will eventually feel confident with these new tasks and not try to go to surrounding objects for security.

Ask for the walk just as you did when leading. In driving, the voice command of the word "walk" or a clucking noise is combined with a loosening of the rein. Your horse should move forward. If so, praise your horse. Keep the horse moving forward by using the command "walk" and praise. If the horse fails to move forward on the walk command, a light tap on either side behind the belly band and above **the trace should start it** moving. **Repeat the command "walk" followed by praise or reprimand** as appropriate.

Make very wide turns at this step. If tight turns are required, lead your horse through the turn and go back to ground driving on the straight-away. Remember to **use half-halts**

(as described earlier) in the turns, giving with your fingers and praising the horse when it turns. **Praise your horse** when he or she walks forward. Do not work on stopping too much in this step. The important thing now is to continue to **walk forward at an even stride.**

STEP THREE: GROUND DRIVING
Stopping & Standing

Ground drive your horse to make sure it understands moving forward on command. In this step, you will introduce the "whoa" command while ground driving. To signal the halt, use the voice command **"whoa"** and gently draw up on the reins. You may find your horse responds better if you use "half halts" (described earlier) with both hands prior to a steady pull on the reins. Release rein pressure when the horse complies.

Practice standing quietly, and starting with the word "walk," and promptly stopping with the word "whoa." If your horse is uncomfortable standing quietly, stop for only brief periods of time and gradually increase the standing time. Verbally praise the horse for standing quietly.

Emphasize the "whoa" command throughout this step. Vary the location of and time interval between halts so your horse will not anticipate the command. Remember, a horse must stop completely and quietly at the word "whoa". Only use that word when you want that response. If you want the horse to move slower, use the word **"easy"** or some other voice command to calm and slow the horse.

STEP FOUR: GROUND DRIVING
Turning

Add side checks in this step if you anticipate driving in breed shows (see Figure 3). If you expect to drive in American Driving Society competition, we recommend not using any type of check unless your horse absolutely needs it. Ground drive again, working on all previous items.

In this step you and your horse spend the most time on less wide **turns** and doing the **figure eight.** Start with large circles and as the horse becomes more accustomed to turning, **make these loops smaller.** Try to make the loops of the figure eight perfect circles. We use the command **"come around"** when we ask for a tight turn. Others use the draft horse terms **"gee"** (right turn) and **"haw"** (left turn).* Praise your horse as it yields to the turn. A tap of the whip on the inside ribs (right sides, if turning right; left side, if turning left) may help the horse to bend and / or move forward in the direction of the turn. Occasionally, the horse may need to be tapped with the whip on the outside shoulder (the side that is away from the direction being turned) to keep the horse from falling outside of the circle.

AMERICAN DRIVING SOCIETY HARNESS
Figure #3

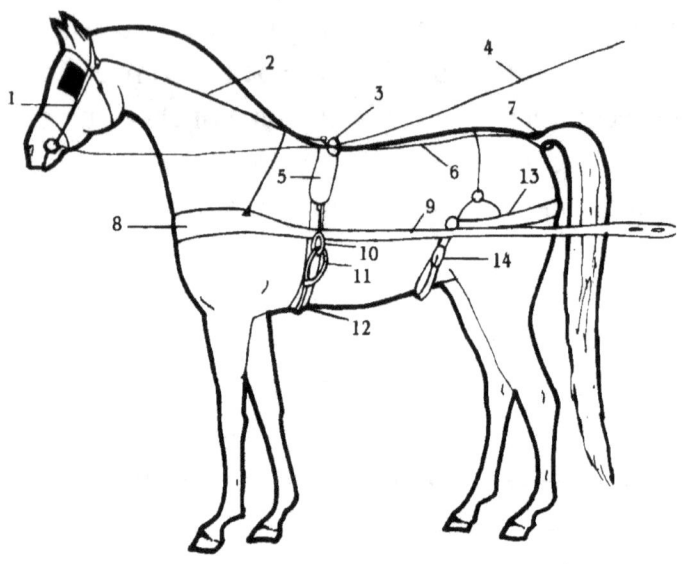

1. Bridle
2. Side Check
3. Rein turret
4. Rein
5. Backpad
6. Back Strap
7. Crupper
8. Breastcollar
9. Trace
10. Shaft Loop
11. Hold Down (Wrap) Strap
12. Belly Band (Surcingle)
13. Breeching
14. Holdback or Breeching Strap

Since your horse may want to stop when using the "half halt" pressure, be sure to give the command "walk" or "walk on" so that the horse moves forward. **MOVING FORWARD DURING ALL TURNS IS VERY IMPORTANT.** You could have **many problems if your horse gets stuck in a turn** by stopping or even worse, backing up. Your cart could overturn.

CAUTION: At least one to two weeks of daily ground driving sessions are recommended prior to attaching a cart - but each horse is different. **Do not advance from this step until you and your horse are confident about all aspects of ground driving in harness.**

*Some drivers use **"get"** for the right turn and **"come"** for the left turn*

STEP FIVE: ATTACHING THE CART

This is the step in which **you need a second person** to help you. Get your cart out and **let your horse examine and sniff the cart.** Then, in your ground driving position, ask the horse to stand quietly while your **assistant noisily pulls the cart in a circle around your horse.** Be sure to praise your horse for not moving and to reprimand it with a sharp "whoa" or "stand" if it moves.

Ask the horse to walk, have your assistant **pull the cart beside the horse, bumping one shaft against it** at approximately the place the shaft will rest when hitched. Do this on each side of the horse. During this step, keep the cart out of the horse's sight and make noise. While your assistant is handling the cart, you **concentrate on your horse moving forward correctly,** praising it whenever possible.

Now you **put the cart to the horse.** Elevate the shafts of the cart before pulling the cart to the horse. Lower the shafts down over the horse's back and place the shafts in the shaft loops. This procedure reduces the chance of poking the horse with the shafts or of the horse stepping on a shaft.

Align the tips of the shafts with the points of the horse's shoulders. The shaft loops should be adjusted so the shafts are slightly higher at the points of the shoulder than at the rump of the horse.

When your horse is settled, jiggle the cart side to side. Ask the horse to stand quietly. Praise the horse for standing.

We **attach the traces to the single tree** first. Adjust the traces so the shafts of the cart are at the horse's shoulders when the traces are taut. Then attach the breeching straps through the loops on the cart (see Figure 4). Lastly, attach the hold down straps. The **hold down straps** are sometimes forgotten. Remember, these straps prevent the shafts from coming up in the air when weight is placed in the cart. They also serve as the brake when no breeching is used. Move the cart forward and backward while the horse is standing to make sure the breeching and breast collar are not too slack nor too tight. If they are too slack, the straps will slap the horse with too much force when it goes to move forward or stops. If they are too tight, they will constrict the movement of the horse.

ATTACHING THE HARNESS AND CART
Figure #4

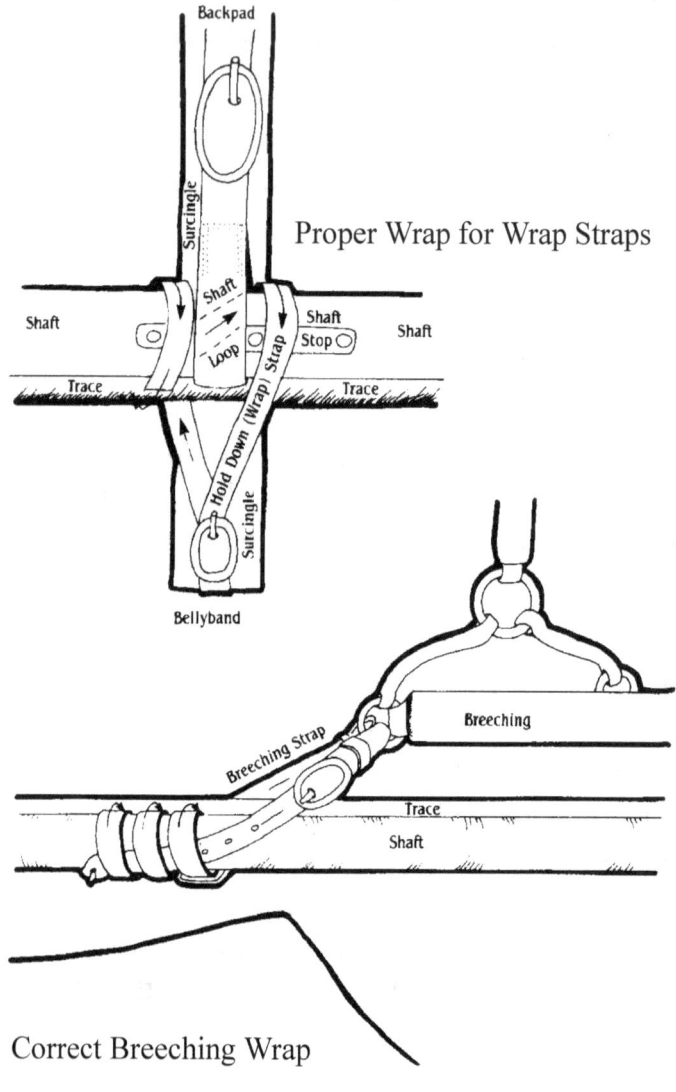

Proper Wrap for Wrap Straps

Correct Breeching Wrap

CAUTION: Be prepared to control the horse should it be unsettled by the new experience of bearing the weight of the cart. Your assistant should have a lead on the horse and be ready if needed.

Ask your assistant to actively **lead the horse** while you walk behind the cart, with the reins in your hands, giving verbal commands, as you did when ground driving without the cart. Your assistant can begin by guiding your horse through your commands, but should gradually take a less active role. To do this, your assistant should **extend the lead line,** and walk farther back, closer to the cart wheels and out of the sight of the horse. If the horse becomes uncomfortable, ask your assistant to go back to leading and then gradually back off from an active role again as the horse becomes more confident.

Stay on level ground at this time. Make very wide turns until the horse becomes accustomed to the feel of the shafts against the sides of its body.

Perform all of your usual starts, stops and turns in both directions and also ask the horse to stand quietly.

Detach the lead line and continue with all of your usual starts, stops and turns in both directions and also ask the horse to stand quietly **but keep your assistant handy in case of difficulty.**

IMPORTANT: Use a two-wheeled cart for all initial single horse training. Only move to a four-wheeled carriage when your horse has learned to stand quietly and only backs the required number of steps.

STEP SIX: GROUND DRIVING
Pulling & Holding Back

Hitch your horse to your cart and, on level ground, practice turns, stops, starts, and standing quietly while you walk behind the cart.

Ground drive your horse at a **walk up and down slight inclines.** Assist the horse by having the assistant either holding or pushing the cart as appropriate. Encourage forward movement and gradually get the horse used to pulling and holding back the full weight of the cart. The assistant may need to lead your horse or hold the weight of the cart.

Give your horse more rein going uphill because a horse must lower his head for pulling. Use the command **"walk up"** or **"pull"**. When going downhill, support the horse by holding the reins more tautly and do not let the horse rush down the hill. Say **"easy"** while applying pressure on the reins and let your horse hold back the weight of the cart with the breeching. Practice ground driving stops, starts, turns, pulling uphill and holding back downhill until your horse is comfortable with the increased weight of the cart.

Practicing Ground Driving at Roadside

Do not leave the designated work area until you and your horse are **confident about commands in harness.** Once both of you have achieved such confidence, you may wish to vary the space in which you train and practice. Move to roadside when your horse is ready for this challenge.

Lead your horse along a roadway without the cart, starting and stopping periodically. Auto and truck noises may startle your horse at first. But, if you stay relaxed and use the word **"easy",** the horse will realize that these noises will not hurt.

Once the horse is quiet while being led near traffic, **ground drive him along the same roadway without the cart.** Most states require that you stay on the right side of the highway moving with traffic. (A slow moving vehicle sign is required when a cart is used on a roadway.) Obey all traffic signs and get your horse accustomed to stopping at intersections.

Signal your turns. For a right turn, extend your right arm while pointing your whip to the right. To signal a left turn, rotate your right arm over your head so that the whips points to the left. To signal a stop, extend your right arm parallel to the ground and point your whip upward at a 90 degree angle.

STEP SEVEN: ENTERING THE CART

At this step, it may not be necessary to ground drive your horse without the cart at the beginning of the session. But be sure the horse is very comfortable pulling the cart through turns, stops, starts, and inclines before moving on to this next step.

Sit on the back of your cart with your legs on the outside. (Be ready for a quick dismount. The training cart should be constructed so you can dismount quickly. You may wish to have an assistant available during this step to stand ready to lead the horse.) Practice starts, stops, turns, etc., in the quick dismount position.

As you and your horse feel more confident, rotate and **sit properly in the seat.** Practice starts, stops, turns, and inclines. If your horse gets frustrated when making turns, it may be necessary to stop, get out of the cart and lead the horse through the turn. This procedure may also be necessary when going through water, over a bridge or by other obstacles. Eventually the horse will be accustomed to these situations and go through the obstacle or turn without your dismounting the cart.

Do not drive your horse with the cart along the roadway unless you are thoroughly confident your horse will not be distracted by any noises or confusions of the roadway.

STEP EIGHT: TROTTING ON STRAIGHT-AWAY & TURNS

This step has two distinct parts; consider using two sessions.

Hitch, and drive your horse while sitting in the cart properly, repeating all previous commands.

On a **level straight work area,** ask for a trot. This is achieved by slightly loosening the reins with the verbal command **"trot,"** then regaining contact with the mouth as soon as the command is obeyed. If your horse fails to trot on command, repeat the command and tap its side with the whip at the same time. Slow to a walk through any turns that are required. Practice this command several times going from the walk to the trot and back again. It is important that your horse **move at the trot in an even tempo.**

Begin to **trot through the turns.** Keep your horse moving forward at the trot when turning. Be sure that your horse is bending his neck and body toward the inside of the turn. While it is best to achieve the bend without the use of the whip, you may need to use the **whip behind the backpad above the trace on the same side of the horse as the turn.** (This is equivalent under saddle to keeping inside leg pressure on the horse in the turn when you are asking your horse to bend around your leg. In driving, you use the whip to act as your leg and the horse should bend his body and neck around the whip in the direction of the turn.) You may also tap the outside shoulder with the whip.

With practice, your horse will be able to maintain an **even tempo at a trot** along the straightaway and through turns in either direction. Do not allow your horse to break into a canter, as that gait can be hazardous in harness and is generally disallowed in competition driving.

STEP NINE: VARYING GAITS
Extension & Collection

Hitch, enter the cart, and repeat the previous maneuvers making sure that the tempo of the gaits is even.

You are now ready to **ask for extension at the walk and at the trot** ("walk-on" and "trot on", respectively). The extension is a longer stride at the same tempo so that more ground is covered. It is not a quicker cadence. You achieve extension by asking your horse to move forward by clucking and loosening the reins just enough to get extension and then pulling back with the reins so it does not break into a canter.

You can also **work on collection in the trot,** which means to get greater knee and hock action (covering less ground) while keeping the same tempo. You achieve collection by holding the reins more taut while still asking for forward motion with your voice and clucking.

STEP TEN: BACKING

Backing can also be achieved at this point since your horse now **thoroughly understands moving forward.**

You can start by asking your horse to back: first in halter, then while ground driving in harness, then hitched to the cart, and then with you in the cart. You may need an assistant to work at the horse's head during the last backing steps when you are at the reins behind the horse.

The horse must have his **nose in a tucked position and shift his weight to the rear** while backing. Therefore, when you start backing your horse in halter, make sure that his nose is down and tucked. Pull the head down and back toward the horse's chest when you ask for a back. You may need to push the horse backward by either pushing at the shoulder or by pulling on the halter so it applies pressure on the bridge of the nose at the same time you say "back". When your horse responds and takes even one step back, praise him and stop pushing. Gradually try to get at least four steps backward on command and always move forward again after achieving backward movement.

When in harness, it is helpful to think of backing in the following way to prevent pulling or tugging on your horse's mouth. As your horse is standing quietly, take up the slack in your reins as you would to halt your horse. Ask for backward movement with a cluck or the word "back". As the horse goes to move forward, it "meets the bit" in this taut rein position and the horse will respond with movement in a backward direction. Gradually get the horse to take more steps backwards in response to just one "back" command. Seldom in the show ring do you need to back more than four steps and then move forward four steps. So practice four steps backward - halt for 2 to 3 seconds, move forward four steps and halt.

Note: Bending through a turn, extension, collection, and backing are the more advanced aspects of driving. They are more complex than we have described here, but these explanations should give you a good start. You may wish to read more about these items later. Consult a professional if you have any problems.

PLEASURES OF DRIVING YOUR HORSE

Driving your horse can offer you a variety of new possibilities for enjoyment. For some, recreating the 19th century form of transportation offers a quest. Some persons appreciate driving as an art form while others enjoy the sporting competition of the show ring. For many if offers a new way to appreciate the out-of-doors and nature. As we grow older, many of us enjoy the comfort of a cushioned seat to the back of a horse. The challenge of training and working with the noble horse is reason enough to enjoy driving.

The camaraderie among driving enthusiasts is also an appealing aspect. I would recommend joining or starting a local driving club so you can share and further your interest with others.

Enjoy Driving Your Horse!

APPENDIX

SELECTED CONTACTS FOR FURTHER INFORMATION

FEI   Federation Equestrian Internationale
Establishes international rules for driving events
https://www.fei.org/

USEF   United States Equestrian Federtation
Establishes standards for horse shows in the US
https://www.usef.org/

ADS   The American Driving Society
Establishes rules for its driving competitions in the US
https://www.americandrivingsociety.org/

www.ingramcontent.com/pod-product-compliance
Lightning Source LLC
Chambersburg PA
CBHW052124110526
44592CB00013B/1746